T0066853

# My Experiences
## — of a —
# Great Man

# MY EXPERIENCES
# — OF A —
# GREAT MAN

## WIPEY

iUniverse LLC
Bloomington

# My Experiences of a Great Man

*iUniverse books may be ordered through booksellers or by contacting:*

*iUniverse LLC*
*1663 Liberty Drive*
*Bloomington, IN 47403*
*www.iuniverse.com*
*1-800-Authors (1-800-288-4677)*

*ISBN: 978-1-4917-0585-8 (sc)*
*ISBN: 978-1-4917-0586-5 (e)*

*Printed in the United States of America.*

*iUniverse rev. date: 12/12/2013*

To the loving memory of the man who stood in the place of my daddy, the man I always called "Uncle." He was Sammy to some people, Samuel to others, Uncle Sammy to yet another large group, and Dr. Blair or even Brother Blair to many, many others. But to my sisters and me, he was Uncle.

You can't imagine how much saying "Uncle" meant to me. Even if I tried to tell you, you would never understand— unless you'd had the magnificent privilege of meeting this great man.

"Uncle" was Samuel Joseph Blair, my mother's younger brother. As the older sibling, my mother knew that her role was to take care of Samuel and their baby sister, Daphne Walker. My mother protected her brother when they were children, but he told her on more than one occasion, "Don't worry, girl. When I grow up, I will look after you." She would always laugh, saying that he thought he was already a man. In her eyes and mind, she couldn't conceive how this younger brother would ever look after her.

I know my uncle is at peace in the best place ever, with great company. I know he's having a wonderful time working for his Father and keeping his watchful eyes on me and the rest of us.

Thank you, God, for the time you allowed me to spend in his presence. I am blessed to be a member of his family.

Uncle, do continue to rest in peace!

# CONTENTS

# PREFACE

This book is about my experiences with a great man that I have had the privilege to know. It is my way of reminiscing and going through the healing process after the hurt of losing a loved one. As I experience life's ups and downs, I can look at this book and try to overcome just one more day.

Pastors—and men and women of God—profess that nothing happens by accident or coincidence. The writing of this book was destined by God to happen, and it did. On Saturday, May 24, 2008, at approximately 3:36 a.m., inspiration gripped me, and I couldn't fall asleep. This inspiration or "little voice" said to me: "Write a book to honor a great man." This jolted me upright, and I got my notepad and wrote the words down. Immediately I knew whom to write about and what to include in the contents. My thoughts kept flowing, and I kept recording information to be included in the various sections of this book.

The very next day, Sunday, May 25, 2008, at approximately 5:55 a.m., I heard a radio announcer say something like "Publish yourself," and I learned that over 250 authors had used this particular service to get their work on the market.

This is my testimony: this entire project is simply God working around and through me, for I had been pondering the question of how to get the book published if I wrote it.

Thus began my writing days, as God continued talking to me. I first heard him clearly back in December 2000, when I was preparing to leave my beautiful native country of

Guyana in South America to migrate to the United States, the world's most powerful and one of the richest countries in this huge, beautiful world that was created by our Lord God.

# Acknowledgments

First of all, I must give praises, honor, and glory to my Lord God, who is indeed an awesome God! There is none like him. He gave me the idea to write, even as he was making me aware of one of the many blessed and rich talents that he has bestowed on me.

I must thank all my relatives and friends for the support and encouragement they have given me. Although they did not have a clue as to what I was doing, they undoubtedly were willing to assist me. There were times when some of them wondered, "What on earth is she doing taking notes?" But I wanted my project to remain secret, and now I am very proud of the result. Once again, I give my heartfelt gratitude to all those involved in the production of my first book.

Special mention must go out to Darryl Forde, who was surprised when I revealed some information to him. He was very willing to support me and to offer some suggestions. My cousin June Barry has also given me valuable information about some relatives living in England, which I have included in my book.

My dear friend and confidant, Dr. Keith Bunyan, always encouraged me to go ahead and publish what I had written. I must have given him a little hint about the contents of the book, and he said to "be proud and put your work out there."

Grateful mention must be given to Collen Braithwaithe— or C. M. Braithwaite, which is the name she uses on her books—for the valuable information she unselfishly shared with me in helping me to decide which one of the numerous publishers to utilize in the publishing of my books.

Last, but not least, I thank my sister Neibert Wilson—with whom I have shared a house for many years—for all her patience, understanding, grave concern, and great love for me.

# Chapter 1

## Wipey

"Wipey" was a name given to me by my one and only uncle. It was funny that he had a unique way of giving nicknames to my siblings and me. No one but my uncle really called me by that name, even though others were aware of it. It was actually just a combination of the first letters from my first and middle names—Yvonne Pamela—but Uncle turned it into an adorable name that I loved to hear him call me.

Uncle also gave names to my sisters: Neibert was called "Dinky," and Leslyn Wilson-Charles was "Boogie." To this day I have never ever been able to figure out the reasons behind their names, and maybe they themselves don't even know. It could have been something to do with their personalities or something they liked to do. These were my uncle's pet names for us, and I'm sure my sisters enjoyed having Uncle call them by these names, even more than their given Christian names.

# CHAPTER 2

## A Great Man Is Born

A son was born to Valerie Jane Bristol Blair and the late Walter Rupert Cornish Blair on September 26, 1928. He was the second child born to this family, the first being Inez Isabella Roberta Blair, his older sister. This second birth was highly cherished, because (1) it was an addition to the family, (2) it was a boy, and (3) he was already destined for great things in his life.

Back in those days, it was the norm for children to be born at home. Children were born in a hospital only if the midwives, nurses, or doctors of the medical team thought it was a high-risk pregnancy or if they already knew that there were some complications involved.

On a bright, sunny day, Samuel Joseph Blair entered this world in a house facing the Atlantic Ocean near Victoria, a small village on the east coast of Guyana. Approximately eighteen miles away from the capital city of Georgetown, Victoria had been the first village to be purchased by freed slaves many years earlier. In later years, this house became better known to my siblings and me as we frequented it during summer break—or the August holidays, as we called it.

As "Sammy" came into the world, his big sister Inez—also known as Sister Inez, Cousin Inez, Aunty Inez, or Aunty—knew that she had her work cut out for her. On a number of occasions later in life, Inez was told repeatedly by her mother, grandmother, and any other female relatives present that she had to protect and take care of her younger brother. Sammy was a posthumous baby, as his father had died before he was born.

As was the norm in our family, whenever a baby was in the midst, he or she became the main attraction. Everybody fussed over the baby. It was and still is my family's way of showing that they really love and care for others.

# CHAPTER 3

## His Early Years

This little boy was lovingly called "Sammy" by his sisters, Inez Blair and Daphne Walker; his mother, Valerie Blair; and his grandmother, Agnes Bristol. He had a great start in life, although it didn't always seem so at first. He was surrounded by love, and all his cousins and other relatives always expressed their love to and for him.

Sammy grew up with his sister Inez and his cousins. He had so much fun playing and being with them that they often got into lots of trouble, but he was a blessed child. When his mother went to work in the capital city of Georgetown, his grandmother, Agnes, was in charge of him. Sammy didn't see his mother as often as he would have liked, but in those days, parents had to do whatever was best for themselves and their families. Grandma Agnes filled the space of his mom, giving him all the love and attention of a mom, but we all know that nobody loves a person more than his very own mom. When his mother was home, she gave him all the attention and love that she could. It was always a pleasure to spend time with the family.

Sammy and Inez continued to grow up, have fun, and live together as any brother and sister would. They just loved being in each other's company.

When Sammy passed his Junior Cambridge Exam, he was awarded a scholarship to attend St. Stanislaus College, a Catholic high school in Georgetown, to further his secondary education. He moved to Georgetown to live with his aunt Jin (Aunt Janet, Eric Hope's mother), and for the first time, he was separated from his loving sister.

Sammy continued on with his education, and at the end of all the hard work, he graduated with his "School Leaving Certificate." After that, he traveled to the United States to further his studies.

# CHAPTER 4

## His Education, Family, and Family Ties

Sammy's dream was to be of service to people of all walks of life. So when he went to the United States, he studied to become a doctor. Originally, he was to do his studies in physical education. However, he attended the Northern Illinois College of Optometry in DeKalb, Illinois, not far from Chicago. He was successful at his studies and became an ophthalmologist, optometrist, and optician.

Upon the completion of his studies, he returned to Guyana—which was British Guiana at that time—to start servicing his fellow Guyanese. He knew about telemarketing and how to promote his service, and he tried to be a member of as many organizations as he possibly could. That way he would become popular, and his service would develop. One of the organizations that he was affiliated with was the Ancient Order of Foresters.

Sammy met and later wed the beautiful Joyce Fraser, "the girl in the pea-green dress," on February 12, 1956. Sammy and Joyce had a wonderful marriage, and they were so loving and welcoming that in 1961 they opened their home to Inez and her three daughters—ages five, three, and nine months—when Inez lost her husband, Leslie Oswald Wilson, after a brief illness. Mind you, they already had two boys—Peter, age three, and Joseph, six weeks old. I was Inez's nine-month-old baby, Wipey.

That was the type of person Sammy was, so looking out for his sister and her children was no big deal for him. Joyce's heart was so huge, caring, loving, and understanding that she opened her doors and accepted this whole family into her home to live with her own new family. I believe there are few women who would do that, especially for so many years.

By 1970 Sammy and Joyce had four boys: Peter, Joey (as we lovingly called him), Robert, and Bernard. That was a total of four boys and three girls, all living in this house with three adults. People were always amazed by how large this family was, especially those who were unfamiliar with its makeup. Lots of them assumed we were all siblings, and we let them think so. Uncle, as my sisters and I called him, liked it most of all when we were all out together and people would turn around and stare. Sometimes they asked him if we were all his, and of course, he would say yes. That was how he treated us, and we surely enjoyed it.

The fun part of growing up in that large household was that we really didn't have to go out looking for friends to play with. Friends always came to our house, because they knew they would surely find at least one child to play with. Some evenings after Uncle came home, he would go outdoors and play with us. Now that was fun.

I remember one particular night when we were experiencing a blackout, and when Uncle came home, he played hide-and-seek with us. It was not so difficult to find us, because the bright moonlight shone down on us as if God was watching his children from heaven.

Sometime later, we were blessed to hear about the expected birth of a girl, and all seven children were very excited. However, the baby was stillborn, which made us all sad. She was so beautiful and had a full head of hair.

Nevertheless, in 1971 we were blessed with the birth of another girl—none other than Golda Ann Aghiza Blair. Her name was decided upon after a conference among Uncle, Uncle Alwyn Fraser, and Uncle Pat Cumberbatch. I believe they said that the baby looked just as precious as that high-value commodity: gold. Of course, Uncle was delighted that he had finally produced his own daughter, but this did not prevent him from loving the rest of us the same as he had done previously. He was rich with love for us all, and the family ties were getting deeper and becoming even more enjoyable.

# CHAPTER 5

## Batty and Posey

This chapter title goes back to the times of old, when people had to have a *posey*—an enamel container that functioned like a bedpan. People who had outdoor toilets or latrines often kept a posey in their rooms to facilitate getting rid of waste matter in the middle of the night. When they needed to use the posey, their *batty*—posterior, buttocks, backside, or rump—was in direct contact with the posey. Sammy and Inez had grown up using a posey, and even after they had their own individual families, this did not change. Indeed, sharing a posey demonstrated a brother's and sister's true love for each other.

15

As time went by, if Inez had a big decision to make, she always—yes, always—consulted with her brother Sammy first to see how he felt about it. Once he confirmed or approved it, she would go ahead and do it. This was because she completely trusted him and knew he would examine the situation thoroughly from all angles, even if it meant that he had to sleep and pray on it for a while.

Wasn't that the way a batty always met the posey, staying in close contact with each other?

# CHAPTER 6

## Stepping Out

We had been living in Bel Air Park for ten long years, from 1961 to 1971. Imagine living with your in-laws for such a long time, being crowded out of your own space, having a second family present whenever you turn around? How much privacy would you and your family really have?

None of this seemed to be a problem for my family, as far as I knew, but I was only a child. What would I know?

Remember that little brother Sammy had said he would look after his big sister, and he had been doing just that. He had looked after his sister and all three of her daughters as if they were his own. In fact, they *were* his, since he and his wife had not yet produced any girls.

However, on September 7, 1971, Uncle's wonderful, beautiful, more-precious-than-gold daughter was born. At that time, my mother knew what had to be done. Although our presence was still very welcome, even after such a long while, Mummy knew it was time for us to step out and move on to allow the Blairs more privacy. Also, with a new baby, there was need for another room.

So Mummy plucked up the courage to inform both Uncle and Aunty of her plans. After much preamble, we moved from A172 Barima Avenue, Bel Air Park, Georgetown, Guyana, to 36 Norton Street, Wortmanville, Georgetown, Guyana, where Mummy had purchased a house years ago after the death of our father, Leslie Oswald Wilson, in January 1961.

It was really sad to leave, but we endured it—and returned to visit just about every weekend. Since there was no direct transportation from our area of Wortmanville to Bel Air Park, we walked about four miles or more to Uncle and Aunty's house every weekend. We met with them and continued to have a good time, as was our custom.

# CHAPTER 7

## Health Issues: The Long Road Back Home

For many years we continued to live and enjoy the times we spent together. We were always pleased to be having a wonderful time. Of course, God was first in our lives, and he has always brought us through everything.

But Uncle's life took a turn when he began to be bothered with health issues. After continuous examinations and tests, it was discovered that his greatest challenge was caused by his kidneys. He was suffering from a disease called polycystic kidney disease or PKD. At the time it started, we in Guyana lacked knowledge of it. The kidneys got progressively worse over a period of time. In the late 1980s, Guyana was not equipped with the necessary technology to fully treat this disease. Uncle was at a stage of using dialysis and changing his bags often during a twenty-four-hour period, since both kidneys had failed. If he ever encountered a very big problem, he had to either fly to the United States to have the doctors fix it or travel to Barbados for help there.

With time, the disease eventually progressed until Uncle was so ill that in January 1988 he was admitted to the private Davis Memorial Hospital. Later he was transferred to the Georgetown Public Hospital. February came, and he was still there. Uncle spoke of many things during his stay in the hospital. I was surprised—and fooled—when I visited him on February 23, 1988 (our Republic/Mashramani Day). He was so energetic, in such high spirits, and his memory was so sharp that I thought things were finally getting better for him.

Then, when I woke the next morning on February 24, 1988, and while preparing to go to work, I received the worst news of my life. "It is all over." Bernard Blair, my cousin/

brother, spoke these words when he and his mom came to tell us the grave news. I had sensed that something was wrong, for it was unusual for Aunty and Bernard to come over to our house at that time in the morning—and instead of using the front door, they had made their way to the back of the house to use the back entrance.

# CHAPTER 8

## End of an Era: My Full Reaction to His Passing

Here, I am using my brother's words. Yes, my brother Bernard spoke these words to my mother: "This is the end of this era for him." He meant that this was the end of his father's era. I know that this was Bernard's way of trying to get Mummy past her grief to continue living. We all knew of the closeness between these two, these "batty and posey," and we knew that Mummy was wondering how she could continue without him.

It had always been "them two," or "*dem* two," in Creolese or broken English. Mummy knew she was supposed to have looked after him. Now, what would she do, not having that very strong male force helping her through life? She seemed to be coping, because she was not letting it all out, as we know she could do only so well—crying and shouting out.

We all grieved in our own ways. For me it was particularly difficult, because this was the father I had known all my life. He had even been my first employer back in 1977. Then, just when I'd thought and hoped that he was getting better—poof! It was all over.

It got better with time, but it took a long while for it to get better. We tried to talk and laugh about the good times we'd had with him, and there had been some really good times.

For example, one day Uncle had come home to an untidy house, so he got really upset and had us lined up outside his door to be punished. One by one, we went inside the room and closed the door. Then we heard lashes from the belt, and shortly afterward, that child came out, not saying a word to the rest of us. It was very scary, especially since we had never seen Uncle punish us in that way.

Then it was my turn, and being as scared as I was, I went in slowly and sheepishly. The door was closed behind me, and I was told to sit on the bed. Uncle had a talk with me, letting me know that he was disappointed to come home and find the house in that state. Then he took the belt and lashed out at the bed. He was lashing the bed, not me, but the next person waiting in line did not know this. So I came outside, and the next person went in for his share. That continued until the last of the seven children had gone into his room.

Uncle is definitely not forgotten, but I have learned to cope with the loss and move on. In my own secret moments, I do remember him and shed some tears, but I know that he has seen all my successes and failures so far, because he is always there, looking down on me and walking with me as I go through this world with all its challenges. He is also watching and protecting me, as are all those other relatives who have gone before us to prepare a place for when we join them.

# CHAPTER 9

## Life After

Life after the passing of Uncle on February 24, 1988, has been full of ups and downs. I do hope it's more ups than downs, but life goes on, and I just need to be thankful and live my life the best way I can. I need to remember to enjoy life as it goes by, day by day, and to keep trusting God so that he can take on all our worries and burdens.

Since Uncle's passing, we have celebrated the birth of Lynella Allison Charles in the United States on August 30, 1988; the marriage of Bernard and Joan in Guyana on June 28, 1989; the birth of Emily Blair in the United States on November 15, 1994; the marriage of Golda Blair and Wain Gaskin in Guyana on July 23, 1994; and the births in Guyana of Ethan Gaskin on November 13, 1995, and Miriam Gaskin on February 14, 1999. We have also seen the marriage of Dwayne and Monique Osborne in the United States in October 2006. We held our first-ever Moses-Blair family reunion in Canada on August 3–5, 2007, and there we met lots of family members for the first time and really enjoyed being in the presence of each other.

And can you imagine the joy of seeing my mother act almost like a child who has found her prized possession? For the first time in all of my mom's long life, she saw a picture of her own father. My, my, my! God is great! Yes, he is! My mom had always wondered what her father looked like and if she resembled him. She clutched that picture and walked around the grounds as if she had found gold. I know that she also shed some tears, being excited and overwhelmed at finally winning such a prize.

Later, we celebrated the marriage of Donna Hope and Mervyn Morris in the United States on July 18, 2008, and the births of their three daughters: Mya Isabella Morris, born on January 23, 2011, and Makayla Neibert and Madison Pamela Morris, fraternal twin girls who were born on March 9, 2012.

Barbara Ford, the daughter of Edward Blair-Ford, and Clifton (Johnny) Osborne were the proud parents of two sons: Marlon and Dwayne Osborne. Later, Marlon became the proud father of two boys named Daquane and Kobie Osborne. On November 3, 2008, in the United States, Dwayne and Monique Osborne became the proud parents of Nicholas. On September 5, 2012, they also welcomed the birth of their precious little bouncing, beautiful baby girl, Olivia Megan Osborne.

Eben (Joy Griffith)—Evelyn Forde Griffith's daughter—and Ronald Allen were united in holy matrimony in Guyana and have produced Ronden (born in Guyana) and three precious and modest girls (born in Canada). Such a wonderful and truly blessed family. Let us continue to keep praying for them, as they are all going through some challenging times, but here again, God is in control, and by his grace and his mercy, things are definitely improving. Hallelujah!

Linden (Bunny Griffith)—Evelyn's older son—got married, and that union produced a precious girl. We also have witnessed the marriage of Tonia Meredith and Kwabina Griffith—Evelyn Forde Griffith's younger son—on December 7, 2002, in Guyana, and from this union they have gladly welcomed their two children Ayjha and Akaia Griffith, born in Guyana on May 23, 2004, and November 28, 2007, respectively. Kwabina's older daughter is a graceful fourteen-year-old whose name is Melika Griffith, and she was born in Guyana on May 6, 1999.

Another great event we have witnessed is the marriage of Wendell Seyum Forde (Cousin Seyum to my sisters and me) to Cheryl in Canada. They have produced a well-mannered young man who is very determined, assertive, bold, and self-reliant. Devon is indeed loved by all of his siblings (I personally witnessed this), and they will do anything to assist him if ever he needs help. Seyum's other children include Trevor, Darryl, Frank, Clement, Audrey, and Whitney Forde. Trevor's children are Dwain, Iqshak, and Sharifa Forde (born in Canada), and he is now happily married to the beautiful Marcia Forde who lives in Guyana.

Darryl Forde (son of Seyum Forde and one of my favorite big cousins) has been happily married to Selma Figaro Forde for many years now. They opened up their beautiful home in Canada to me in August 2012. It was such a great blessing and honor to have a place to go, and I spent six nights there. Maybe others thought I was overstaying my welcome, but no one made me feel so. Their close friends and other family members welcomed me into their midst, and I truly enjoyed my stay there, which helped me to gather much more information needed for the successful completion of this book.

At Selma and Darryl's house, I had the great pleasure of meeting and spending precious time with Nya Forde. She is the daughter of Whitney Forde and granddaughter of

Seyum and Cheryl Forde. Nya is a beautiful, bold, friendly and loving four-year-old bundle of joy. She takes awhile to warm up to strangers, but when she does, she is a very good playmate. She spends most of her weekends with her Uncle Darryl and Aunty Selma, keeping them busy and definitely on their toes.

Judith Cunningham and Patrick Barry (Muriel Forde's son) wed in Canada and have produced Salina Barry, a very delightful daughter. Now my cousin June Barry (daughter of Muriel Forde) has a son, Nigel Williams (born in Canada), who is married to Kelly Williams, and they too have a wonderful, bouncing son full of energy. Atticus, whom I met for the first time in August 2012, is a very loving child who loves to play with balls, whether it involves throwing or kicking them. Who knows? He may be a future professional athlete! They had the birth of their second son in October 2012, as was expected. I wish them all the very best and God's eternal blessings! I also hope they have lots of energy to keep up with two boys. I look forward to my next visit to Canada, where I can meet this new addition to our growing family.

I really do miss Uncle every day, but I try to stay focused on all the positive things in my life. Since I am only on planet Earth for a short time—the exact amount, I don't know—I need to enjoy the best of it and not worry about the small fishes. I will let God, my Creator, worry about that for me.

Remembered also are the sad moments. I pause to reflect on the lives of Peter Blair (my cousin/brother), who crossed over from this side of the world to the other side on December 31, 1998. I also take time to reflect on Aunty, or Aunty Joyce (Uncle's wife), deceased on March 6, 2002 and Joseph Blair (my cousin/brother), deceased on March 30, 2003.

Some other sad times for me are when I sit down and reflect on my cousin Joy (Eben), who went into the hospital for a simple in-and-out procedure, a colonoscopy, which I myself have had done. (Most women have it done on or

near their fiftieth birthday.) We don't know what happened
to her when she was in the theater, but we surely came very
close—yes, very close—to losing her. Of course, I have no
idea what happened, and I have only heard horror stories
of some of the things she had to endure.

But all honor and glory and power to our Lord God, our
healer, the mighty one! If it weren't for his goodness, his
grace, and his mercies, where would any of us be today? I
have no choice other than to continually thank him, and I
ask that we keep lifting up Joy and her family in our daily
prayers.

Also, I recently found out about another dear cousin,
Glenroy Blair-Ford, who lives in England and met with
an unfortunate accident when he was out on a field trip
with his students. He is now forty-six years old, paralyzed,
and cannot move his body below his neck. He is living in a
residential nursing facility and will have to spend the rest
of his life in a wheelchair.

These are all hard memories to forget or let go of, but as God guides my path each and every day, he continues to make me stronger and helps me to cope with my losses. I so thank him for the precious times I have had with my family and the special things they have imparted in my life.

Thank you, God, for letting me share in their sweet lives.

# CHAPTER 10

## What I Have Learned and
## How Others Have Benefited

Through it all I have learned so much, and I continue to learn each and every day. I am so grateful for having had such a person as Uncle in my life. Both my uncle and my mother came from very humble beginnings, which they have neither forgotten nor felt ashamed of, and they have passed their heritage on to their family.

Over the years, even as my uncle's status in life changed, his attitude and behavior remained the same. Dr. Samuel J. Blair never became a "big shot" or ignored others, nor was he out to become rich at the expense of his fellow men. Because of his Christian upbringing, he never used his profession to try to get rich, as many of the other doctors in his field were doing. In fact, he was known as the "poor man's doctor," simply because he made his services accessible and affordable to the poorest of his people.

I had the great privilege of working with him for over two years and learned a great deal about him and from him, including how to perform some of the technical aspects of the profession. I have seen the goodness of his heart many times when he worked for free and reduced the price of glasses to accommodate people. When families said they couldn't afford to pay for glasses, he gave them glasses without charge. I know he was losing lots of income when he did this, but such generous acts testify to his goodness.

Uncle had his patients read from a small Bible testament to determine whether they were seeing better with their new prescription and were satisfied with his work. Sometimes he asked certain patients whether they read their Bibles daily. Most of these selected ones, if not all, answered with an assertive, "Yes, Dr. Blair!" He would tell them that he read his Bible daily as well. Then he would ask them to locate Psalm 151 and read it before they could go. It was so interesting to see these adults flip through the testament to find the book of Psalms, and then, after skimming through, to discover that there was no Psalm 151, as there were only 150 Psalms. They would laugh and say, "Oh, Dr. Blair, you are too wicked!"

Sometimes, instead of having them locate Psalm 151, he would ask them to read Psalm 119 before leaving the office. If you remember, I said earlier that this was a small testament, so when Uncle gave them the book, it did not seem like a lot to read—for the first two pages. However, when they began to read and read and read and read, they suddenly began to start flipping pages to see where it ended. You can imagine their amazement when they realized that this Psalm was the longest one, having 176 verses. Now, if you were reading your Bible every day, as you say, wouldn't you think you might remember that Psalm 119 is the longest one, or is it just me?

Many other family members benefited directly or indirectly from Uncle's offices in South Road, Lacytown, Georgetown, Guyana, or Alexander Street, Lacytown, Georgetown, Guyana, or Church Road, Georgetown, Guyana. He also had an office in Mackenzie, one of our mining towns approximately sixty-nine miles from Georgetown. Michelle Porter-Bradshaw, Mervyn Morris, and Della Porter all worked either with Uncle at Alexander Street or Church Road or with "Joey" Joseph Blair at his computer school, the Institute of Computer Learning in Georgetown, Guyana.

# About the Author

Yvonne Pamela Morris, formerly Yvonne Pamela Wilson of Georgetown, Guyana, South America, has been an auditor and an educator for a number of years. She currently resides in Fort Washington, Maryland.

She will be penning all her books under the name "Wipey."

Printed in the United States
By Bookmasters